Unhomely
Montage-Machines

Teufel-INK

PREFACE

"We protect our minds by an elaborate system of abstractions, ambiguities, metaphors and similes from the reality we do not wish to know too clearly; we lie to ourselves, in order that we may still have the excuse of ignorance, the alibi of stupidity and incomprehension." Aldous Huxley

Can Truth be arrived at through the imposition of patterns, rules, and methods? Indeed, is there a Truth to be unveiled, within the universe? A curtain to be raised, by Dorothy and her deficient company, to unveil the mechanics of reality? This is perhaps a poor analogy, given that in that film at least, truth is seen ultimately to be the by-product of the machinations of those who know reality is malleable and work it for their selfish ends. Should Truth even be capitalised? Romanticised? Idealised? Singularised? Or is it many truths that shoot up momentarily in a purely relational and subjective union of prejudice and opportunity?

This, far from exhaustive list of conundrums and ponderings, are some of the questions this collection of poetry does not even begin to answer. This is a work of masturbatory mysticism, idiocy, and structure-less perplexity. I am confused, why shouldn't you be too?

Over 21 days, I endeavoured to write 21 poems. Ostensibly giving myself some guiding principle, method, and structure, I drew and reflected upon a Tarot card from the traditional Marseilles deck each day. Focussing on the images on the cards, I wrote out of the images, symbols and titles, often finding myself in unforeseen territories. Formatively, the idea was to give a structural and thematic aid from which to work, yet as the writing continued, I realised that the language that was being generated between myself and the images became less and less anchored in the chosen card; instead the concepts and words became ripped and exposed, a cacophony of syllables that, in truth, belies both the excitement and fear I feel in the face of an infinitely fascinating and infuriating universe.

I am a lie, beguiled by rhythm and ruled by rhyme.

I DREW THE SUN *(Active masculine side. Rational intelligence, energy, vitality, loyalty, courage, and generosity; expression of firmness and stability. Joy, clarity, love, friendship, dazzlement.)* And yet we still dance, looking forward, looking down, to enjoy, to bask, to feel the grass that grows because of what you give. Wreathed in flowers, flares brief, blissful falsities powerful. I only see because of the light you give allows. A brick wall behind me, a certain security of what this was, what this was and what could stop being; foetal, ancient, and forgetful. My collective memory stumbles, imperious, crippled. A duet that has slept and danced with Psyche and Apollo. They have, respectfully, assured us that they will never leave us until we, bandy-legged with unbridled joy reach a point of complete quantum dispersion. (On reaching said coordinates, it is politely, yet firmly requested that we all, hand-in-hand, return to that singular point from which you know you could not have helped but depart). Those rays that hold all colour, all life, all that is life, all gold, now obscured by frosted windows held by all that is limp and old. All that lies through a history of truths untold shine now, do not drip upon pallid skin, mine that craves the warmth promised, not delivered, stolen. Solar trickledown economics that should otherwise be pregnant with excess. I

squint. She squats. I stare at the sun, like we all have done, and see the lustre of gold melt into the flesh-red impoverished eyelids. We burn white before welcoming eternal night. The sun. Your treasures. My piss. These are all toys, the colour of sulphur. **I DREW THE MAGICIAN** *(Represents the beginning and the capacity to grow, dominating the elements. A person in action, lively, gifted in abilities, creativity, charm, and cunning. Youth, security, astuteness.)* I could not stand upon Hasting's shore Feel the wind blow so deeply, resolutely, with all the power of your hateful gales. I could not withstand, as I stood upon that West Hill In my charming neighbourhood, the oncoming storm of perpetual prejudice. Be quiet you winds, stand firm you earth, Be still the fire that boils water already disturbed. Be still, hold firm, be Heart be Soul; be fervent in ideal and let love for all not stir. Let me not forget, that I pulled Death and put him back. Let me not forget I then drew the Fool and turned him back. Why was that? Because we are Magicians, We have power over the Pack. **I DREW THE CHARIOT** *(Capacity to choose which direction to take. An adventure, the courage of those who know what they want, flaunting. Success, travel, control, determination, triumph.)* Crown'd and scepter'd I stand, holding no reigns For the Beasts that tear me apart, Under a ruling canopy of stars. A spectre, a burden. Crown'd and scepter'd, I fall beset and besieged by the unbearable weight of impossible, endless choice. For four eternal days I have again been locked in by my endlessly open doors. It is within this space, made liminal by the forces of nostalgia and unease, That I wait to see what I myself will make of me, and watch the hours, the days, the years Slip serrated through possibilities. For myself and in myself; gnossienne. A little house, underground, all the trappings of a home but cold, dark, weird. Here is the main road, Here, the way out; a garden, a water park, a kitchenette, and car storage. This little house of Becomings Exacerbates sensuality, All things occurring at once; Nerves flooded by pleasure and pain Forever Oscillating in Lacanian jouissance. My eyes are inverted and my stomach sits like a sphere rotating upon a pin-point totem pole, rising higher, until it unfolds itself like a flower bud. Like a flower bud, I cascade back upon me, Cradling my body with anther; Lifting me up, pulling me back into ovaries, In which I gestate, Grow again, and again, Repeat the process. **I DREW THE BELOVED** *(Capacity to choose; a fork in the road where the one of two options must be decided. Feelings, love, a love triangle. Choice, trust, falling in love, indecision, balance.)* Lands once broken, now will rise up against those chosen by themselves to pin us down. Come earth, come dirt, and bury that false crown that steals from her people with tricks and feints. And is it us that dances in bright paints? And is it us to build this paper town upon our beloved England's wise ground? Blessed heads of tissue Saints do disappoint. No ground will be out of bounds to fresh minds Eager to renew that which we had lost. No breath further to be taken from us if taken from us to enslave mankind. Don't build Jerusalem at any cost, Earth, once pure; for wealth and war used; now cursed. I **DREW THE HIEROPHANT** (*Capacity to go beyond the material aspect of things. Authority that resides in spiritual power; a figure capable of being an intermediary between two worlds. Spirituality, vocation, guidance, wisdom, mediation.*) I would rather than Hierophant be, An Acephale living for and in ecstasy; to escape rather than abuse thought to Develop a relationship with the One or Many believed to have created us. I renounce the state, the grey suits of formality and vice, and so too I renounce the Church and their indentured, diminished mice, I renounce all and everything that will try to reduce the universe and all myriad life to an extension of itself. Follow still, and dance with the Headless; agitating the void. Shake shackles of function and set fire to reason. For, in that system that 7 Tears us apart for servitude to capital lies the truth of long-buried Theseus; That Labyrinth, the Minotaur, and the favoured son are one - A hermetically sealed prison cell that secures none.

I DREW THE HANGED MAN (A

moment of stagnation, when nothing is getting done. Propensity to sacrifice, a change of perspective. Deprivation, spiritual elevation, victimism, initiation, betrayal.) Suspended in this moment - A moment drawn complete By Mnemosyne and Aion, when they finally never meet. A moment reversed, perpetual, constant, and indefatigable Like the Ouroboros, the eternal prey preyed upon eternally by itself; The snake rejuvenescing, bathing in tempests of time; Like the abysmal image of the depths made topless, Like the Möbius strip and bottles of Klein: I am lost in two dimensions yet I feel fine. My heart is above my mouth, and it pours out. I shout, only to find my toes tremble. If I could ask to be reassembled, reconstituted, and reformed 9 to start my day again, I would not, I am content upside down. And was it you who drew these ropes about my feet? You who sculpted me into this Borromean knot with one tree with life replete the other's life excreted? Was it you who hitched me to this branch, demanding complicity? Who said, disbelievingly, suspend disbelief? The veil slips from my eyes finally Due to invariable forces intent on trapping me and in so doing, set me completely free. I am, as I hang, neither on the ground nor with Celestials, A transcendental axiom in and of myself: Entirely self-sufficient, A terror to myself, yet rigorously immanent alongside the real as I am ejected ex uterine into the engine of perpetual invention. So here I swing, a thing with mechanics exposed, Augmented, unforeseen, and full of possibilities, Ungoverned and structureless, When immanence and transcendence, Hybridised, dyadic, Consumed and consummated, my senses slithered in perpetual displacement. I have, as I hang, no point of departure or arrival No death drive nor sense of survival. No singular god-head as an object of meditation, just a sublime, continuous recapitulation. I am an Abbey of Crime I am a library of unwritten pages, in which both monk and beast have fucked throughout the ages. I have, as I hang, confounded space I have, as I hang, confounded time, Non-materialisation, non-territorialisation. Simply through methodologies of forgetfulness and idiocy. I am, as I hang, not distinct from my other my interior is synonymous with your exterior, though approached in mirror form. I have, as I hang, neither lived nor died Seen nor did unseen Please never let me be untied. **I DREW THE HIGH PRIESTESS** *(The power of knowledge and receptive feminine knowledge. A phase during which importance is given to reflection, to accumulating knowledge. Wisdom, intuition, reserve, mystery.)* And what still day is born, Through the Sapphic union of the crescent silver moon and precious spectrumed dawn? What balance cradled, what calm held over violent seas, untouched by the faintest breeze? These waters unsullied by Romantic's lusty oars that leaves no shore unkissed nor forlorn, but pregnant, if pregnant be: A moment rebirthed in eternity, a reflection not retreating, nor staking false claim to lands founded in blood and held for profit or fame. **I DREW THE STAR** (*Hope. Following one's vocation, living in harmony. Situation in which one feels at peace and in synch with their own nature. Beauty, far-sightedness, desires, following one's own path.*) Please guide me through this... We can't be with you right now But, I could really do with a little... Your call is very important to us I need to say something poignant, I have only a few... You are 13th in the queue Thalia, please pick up, there is a forest I would love to summon up in imagery Press 5 for customer service Erato, then, please how do I write a swollen heartbroken? Press 4 for technical issues Polyhymnia, then, if this poem is of stars, please.... If you would like to speak to a member of our team, say "yes" Yes I'm sorry, I did not hear that, if you would like to... Yes. Yes! All of our operatives are otherwise engaged, please hold. FFS. **I DREW JUDGEMENT** (*Rebirth, a calling, reawakening. A new phase of life, definitive and irreversible renewal. Capacity to be ready to change. Calling, manifestation, repentance.*) A fire, in devastating waves, ripped through Old Town last night. Decrepit timbers, long-seeking renewal, razed Slipping through midnight ash. And you all stood around, ogling the destruction like it was the 90s and you, you were on your tea break with Page 3 Sipping another milky cup of tea as this scepter'd isle Took another slump in its economy. "And why the inferno now?" Rose the jeers "When, like a knock-kneed beggar, unmoving this building has remained for years Sealed off with scaffolding on the edge of under cliff avenue." No impetus to change, in Britain now, unless for reasons of lost revenue, "No need", they said, as homes and hearth were bled, "To feed a sickly cow before bolting it through its head." I DREW JUSTICE *(The need to find balance, equity, and impartiality. Capacity to make judgements, situation, the right person or decision. Equilibrium, harmony, law, logic, impassibility.)* When your house is stricken, your last card played, Think of God and how despite this, He is neither moved nor seeks to move. Come rain, come storm, Come across young lives stolen and torn, Think of Him and take warmth; nothing that you suffer through will touch your Lord - Impassible as He is. Impassibility is an archaic idea, which, as I read, seems to mean a complete lack of empathy... So, here's His Church, here's His steeple; Unfeeling stone, cold steel, unheard people. I will brook no sociopathic celestial being to govern a universe, in which the primacy of pleasure and pain undoubtedly reigns. No god for me, who does not feel the love, the hate, and all between, felt so keenly through a life in which He demands we serve. I DREW THE UNNAMED CARD (*Death and rebirth; change and transformation. Invitation to manifest one's own essence, without superstructures, paying attention only to the essential. Cut, end, loss.*) Seems strange to reduce to the singular, a battle invariably lost against entropy. It is the insta-story ego versus the second law of thermodynamics. It is Jesus holding back ΔS. Mohammed sweeping dirt under the rug. Buddha frantically cleaning the crime scene before we notice that, exsanguine the body lies. I drink to a plethora of gods the possibility of an endlessly variable anima, to forgetting who I was before I become something other, over again and over again. To the big toe clenching in the dirt. To my pineal eye bursting. To my stomach, which is swollen, containing a vast maze of libraries written in languages of which my tongue cannot still yet conceive. So no, not one. Many. Cry disorder and dispersion set out screaming, breaking the firmament open with joy and laughter. My joy, my laughter, a knife through the heart of the scion, Who has, with his scythe-like heirlooms, Gathered our myriad wealth and gathered for only himself. So no, not one, Many. So no, not one, Many. I DREW THE FOOL THEN I DREW THE

HERMIT *(The Fool is the only Arcanum without a number. The man who continues along his path of evolution leaves reason behind to allow his creative energy to express itself. Joy, enthusiasm, freedom, madness, innocence —— —— The Hermit: wisdom, research, relationship with time, old age. A period when there is a need to look inward and spend some time alone. Prudence, silence meditation, hermitage, widowhood.)* Joy – Prudence The landscape seems to extend infinitely... The sky too... Vast and indecipherable, into the space pour tears – Space tears and ruptures – As we reintroduce ourselves. The movement of the air that flew undisturbed is excited and jostled by our presence; it slows and sweeps around, investigating the new agent. Weep for the lost horizon. A Fool on a journey to meet a Hermit, Who cautions against frolicking. Enthusiasm – Silence and still, these images taunt me with their wilderness and confident loneliness. Their peaks and valleys rise and fall like economic graphs: All meet the smooth eternal stretch of deep blue and sky blue, striated space and striated finances that will be when we return, not as they used to be. Towards equality and unity, we march, in our solitary cells. A Hermit waits for a Fool; Begins to rupture the silence in enthusiasm. Freedom – Hermitage I have data fatigue. Statistics, graphs, and charts have disassociated me. I check the figures daily and see The abstracted numbers of 933 More dead: 933 More intricately connected lives, Interweaved with exponentially more other lives Who in turn.....who in turn: Where n equals someone you do not know multiplied by y (Someone who is left behind). "I am free," says the Fool, bound for the Hermitage. Madness – Meditation. I think well when I am travelling; for the moment no movement. I will take your figures and cartographise you; each incremental increase moves me across the earth to a different location, both real and imagined – The digital realisation of mathematical abstraction. I find myself in the deserts of In Amguel. I find myself in the Kara Sea, in Xudun, In the Gulf of Guinea, Seychelles, Tchirozerine, And the Norwegian Sea. Cadaveric cartographies move me closer to your realities. We are still connected – I travel so that you are remembered. The Hermit has sat silent, meditating, awaiting the madness of his friend, the Fool. Innocence – Widowhood Rock formations spring up like couch grass. Franny recounts a dream: "There is a desert". She said. Smooth space meets a vast geological rupture, these cliffs leak into the sea. These vast, vast walls meet the cold, cold waters and these cold, cold waters meet the blue, blue sky – A striation of space made beautiful through its leakages. Writing itself unfolds like a camel ride, with unpredictable speeds, slownesses, spurts, and stoppages. A gulf. Not a void. Instead a space in which, two forces embrace and unify. This is not an abyss, nor is it a difference that separates and classifies; it is a plateau on which the velocity of a vast body of water Caresses and communicates with the land which in turn has its own paths moulded and altered accordingly. A multitude of islands, a conglomerate of platforms interconnected out-croppings. Strata meet strata meet strata Then they fall away only to rise again. We are archipelagos in ourselves: Not continuous lands, we are ever inconsistent but consistently rise in Surprising architectures of being. The spaces between these architectures are the true frames of fascination. The Fool had not realised, the Hermit had lost his wife. I DREW THE GOD HOUSE *(Change, revelation. Breaking free of something that was keeping you prisoner; possibility to manifest oneself. Sudden events. Creative energy, lack of control, collapse, fear.)* The plans drawn up, permission granted a tower was built, but slightly slanted, torn down again, and again restarted whilst families evicted and broken-hearted sat asking, for shelter and safety from the men paid repeatedly for basic necessities. These towers will be built for all of us so said the slogan on the side of the bus so do be patient, do wait in turn to live in towers built to burn. I DREW TEMPERANCE *(Balance, gentility, attention. Patience, perseverance and measurement; capacity to combine different energies when moving forward, moderating instincts. Harmony, stagnation.)* We sat down, like many times before, Round the kitchen table, food eaten, wine poured. We set about breaking the week apart; how did it end? Usually worse than the start. She slipped through her thoughts, sporadically Falling across an infinity of "oh, and anotherthings…" I thought I sat there quite patiently, until I felt my leg jigging up and down tremulously; keep focussed, I said to me, and try to not interrupt… But, I want to reply before I have forgot. "Don't be abrupt…. Let me just finish… God I can't get a word in edgeways" She says after I uttered, one syllable dazed and lonely. "Well, fine, then, go on, if you must." It's just, I've been trying to write more and would love to share my thoughts with you, as no one else will care. I'll speak them out if that helps? You don't have to read. "Okay, then, but do hurry" I read them out; words that had been bled from me; On beauty, on pain, on random philosophy, On everything that came to mind first Caught in meter, wrapped in verse. "You don't put any emotion into speaking, it's dull, your voice." And, with no choice, the words grabbed from my mouth "Here's how you do it" She began to read so eloquently Just like you're supposed to do with poetry. "See? That's how you do it, now, back to me." I hope one day you'll hear me again know the words of love and fire and soul within but how would you, Em? You'll never bloody read them. But, on the off chance that you do, just as a post-script, a note to the one on whom I do truly dote, know that poetry often deals with imagined insecurities, Broad brushstrokes, subjective realities, see? Paints a life rife in ironies, believe me? Because she never really said what I wrote and I suppose it's best not to write, when I've been sleeping on the sofa for three cold nights, my spine bent into a question mark, like the questions, I wish she'd ask me about all my endless thoughts and endless endless, endless fucking poetry. **I DREW THE EMPEROR** *(Self-confidence and material security. A phase of tranquillity, a mature figure, a role of power, self-reliance. Stability, authority, concreteness, decision, power.)* There's a bric-a-brac shop on St Leonard's seafront, Sells odds and ends, furniture, lamps, And HandMeDowns. Flamboyantly calls itself "20th Century Art and Design", But it's just stuff no one really wants. Three floors deep, chthonic, past art deco-mirrors sloganned with dated images of buxom wenches having pints of Guinesses, "Just the tonic!" Or would-be, should-be, toothless kids Smiling with bottles of coke unlidded Past rows of moth-eaten military jackets, Cracked vases and ashtrays Sullied opaque with sentimental touch And hacking coughs. In the depths, past it all, upon the cracked paint of an unlit wall Framed, famed, and most imperious; there's Vladimir Ilyich Uyanov,

Statesmanlike portrayed, Looking out over his new land and waiting for that red wave, To wash upon his new shores, Shores peopled with unwanted memorabilia. His power forgotten, his image orphaned, but his words, resonating with us, the bargain-hunters, the canlhaveabitoff's and the whatsthebestyoucando's cos it's just like Lenin said: "I am the Walrus." I DREW THE EMPRESS *(Ideas that become fertile and create; an action already underway and ready to bear fruit. Capacity to love; fertility, a true pregnancy. Practicality, decision, power and intelligence.)* It was after all this... Albion, throned and moneyed. It was during this... 3.9 million children below the poverty line. It was after all this... You broke our families. Perfidious Albion You have broken trust. Perfidious Albion you have left us lost. Perfidious Albion Leaders never voted. Perfidious Albion, Liars in luxury. Lives hard-fought for, lie in tatters under your golden-heeled boots. I DREW THE MOON *(Feminine receptive side. Intuitions, dreams, sensitivity, emotions, memories, receptiveness, instinctive part, hidden things. Mystery, ambiguity, passivity.)* I saw the truth, stepping from my door Reflected in the sea, I swore I saw the truth, a lobster aggressing the shore. Two dogs, lost, howling at you, as they caught coloured petals in their jaws. And you, the truth, shining up from the water; through changing each day, from pregnant sphere to sabre-curve, Remained, constantly changed. And in me too, reflected from some sacred depth A changing voice, consistent, still swarmed on my breath Fluctuating and nomadic – a life of glorious inconsistency. And what do I feel this is? Dared. Dreaded.

De

     bil

         itate

         d.

And I guess that I am here. Could you not jump, if you wouldn't mind? Could you? Stop filming. Stop filming. Across the waterway, barely demarcated by Google maps. Smash him in the face. You did it. Shout. Walk up a hill. Feel justified. And that carriage is late again. 5 minutes – just in time so I taught you 3 years ago, I thought you would think....? It is as it has been thought to have been, but they said they did it for you. Shuffle. Shuffle. Nothing moves. Joy of a child. Stopped. Not comforted – your own. Bang. Zoom Shuffle. Shuffle. ZOOM. Bang. Don't you fucking know who I fucking am? I DREW THE WHEEL OF FORTUNE (The ups and downs of life; a cycle in perpetual motion, ability to accept one's destiny: a stroke of good or bad luck.

Destiny, chance, conclusion, fate.) My heart aches and the Fool steals off with joy. My sense, as though dulled and drowned in the sand is conned by Magicians, now redeployed to steal your life, a friend wrenched from my hand. Tis' not through envy of High Priestesses, But being lost in Dalston again my friend, That you, wheel-spinning, keep me down here In some jail of Empresses' Of locked doors and bleached hallways with no end; An Emperor, now dethroned cries havoc. No Hierophant will allow me access To a mind lost in tragic accident Lovers we were if love is art professed, Danced, Kafka through the night, wine-kissed, well-meant Stop that Chariot crashing through my dreams, Full of possibilities dispossessed, With bold Strength ripping wild beasts' jaws apart, And shadow struck seems; Not Hermit born, but left, nevertheless, Yet still not faded in my scratching memory: The Wheel of Fortune brings me back to you What scattered writings of yours still unknown, No Justice, armed, blind, swords swing at the few No this way or that, signs unseen, unshone; Where I, upside down, a Hanged Man, strung, done Where my face grows pale, and sorrow-full dies; Where unnumbered death sits eating your problems And floating joy moves on, Where Temperance cannot keep her calming eyes, For new balance lies when stolid hearts condemn. Away! Away! I will not Devil draw Not charioted by decision unmade Towers are built and built to be unsure, A love for a people, a love in shade: And I am taken along by the Star, She guides me, simultaneously One Silvered Moon cuts through; eyes, grey clouds, and spoons; But here there is no light, But I still, since you've gone stared into the Sun Through a life too quickly taken, a life undone. The Judgement I make, though not through my feet Says much of those friends that fall from now, The World, it's ours made incomplete I come back to you an ally avowed. A Nightingale, Daniel, fell far from the roof, A Nightingale, Daniel, fell far from the crowd. I DREW THE DEVIL *(Restrictions. Dependence on something or something. Constrictions that provoke anger. Personal magnetism. Sensuality and sexuality, total lack of self-control. Psycho-physical energy.)* Lost son, fallen, built Banks deep in the broken hills; stripped fruit trees bare. I DREW THE WORLD *(Obtaining something you desire. Perfection, harmony, wholeness among the different aspects of existence. The desired result, happy closure of a cycle, attaining one's desires.)* I drew the world today, though not a perfect circle, Drew too, those cradled within arching arms, uncertain As blindly they sat, both breaking and mortal, Feeling that her rough skin drew back, uncurtained; They touched the flesh of undulating earth Prostrate and languorous before them. She wept for cold scars made centuries deep, and was seen trembling throughout still lighted night. But did she wail for dreams harmoniously failed? No; it was us in great pains wracked by life ungrown. Listen, you captains of industry, hear wind-born cries as you tear her asunder. Her belly you mined her lungs sullied, her heart irreparably plundered. So now to join, at least on paper, two points drawn of an imperfect circle. We have not, with loving arms gathered, she who likewise lovingly gathers; our time is up, but hers is not as all life stretches from her womb, for we, who sought to profit; now alone entombed. I DREW STRENGTH (*Courage that wins over brute force and over instincts; victory that can be attained with intelligence without using force. Physical and psychic energy, instinct, lucidity, control.*) I am only left with strength, After all this, Strength to see what comes; Strength to wake and live Strength to hold the hand that needs a tender guide through Heaven-born winds. Nibble-nibble-gnaw-gnaw the wind, the wind. And so my house still stands, built to last as long as us, and no more, Nothing I need needs to persist longer than that. Strength to be fragile to fail and in failing, stand, not fallen. Remembered for as long as memory comforts or intrigues.

Printed in Great Britain
by Amazon

22940458R00020

Unhomely
Montage-Machines

Teufel-INK

Printed in Great Britain
by Amazon